EARTHWORM

By Lee Jacobs

**BLACKBIRCH®
PRESS**

THOMSON

GALE

San Diego • Detroit • New York • San Francisco • Cleveland • New Haven, Conn. • Waterville, Maine • London • Munich

Photo Credits: cover © Getty Images; pages 3, 4, 5, 6, 7, 8–9, 10–11, 12–13, 14, 15, 18 © CORBIS; pages 16–17 © Corel Corporation; pages 20, 21 © Dwight R. Kuhn Photography; pages 22–23 © PhotoDisc

LIBRARY OF CONGRESS CATALOGING-IN-PUBLICATION DATA

Jacobs, Lee.
 Earthworm / by Lee Jacobs.
  v. cm. — (Wild America)
 Includes bibliographical references.
 Contents: The earthworm's environment — The earthworm body — Predators — The mating game — Earthworms and humans.
  ISBN 1-56711-568-3 (hardback : alk. paper)
  1. Earthworms—Juvenile literature. [1. Earthworms.] I. Title. II. Series: Jacobs, Lee. Wild America.

QL391.A6 J33 2003
592'.64—dc21   2002015837

Printed in China
10 9 8 7 6 5 4 3 2 1

Contents

Introduction

Earthworms have lived on earth for 120 million years. They can be found in most parts of the world. As long as they can burrow into the ground and stay out of the hot sun, earthworms can live almost anywhere.

Earthworms belong to the phylum (scientific group) Annelida, which is made up of segmented worms. These worms have bodies that consist of many segments, or parts. Other types of segmented worms include leeches, bristleworms, and ragworms.

Leeches (top) and ragworms (bottom) are related to earthworms.

There are about 2,700 different kinds, or species, of earthworms. They are classified into five families. Some tropical species live in water. But most live in the earth, as their name suggests. Earthworms found in North America are part of the family Lumbricidae.

The Earthworm's Environment

An earthworm's environment is the ground. In just 1 acre (0.4 ha) of soil —a little less than the size of a high school football field—there may be thousands of earthworms. Earthworms live in the ground in many kinds of habitats. Although they are all different, these habitats share something in common. They all have places that are dark and damp. That is because earthworms need moisture to live. The hot sun will dry out an earthworm and kill it.

Earthworms live in burrows. To dig these burrows, earthworms eat the soil and excrete, or get rid of, the waste as they move along. How deep an earthworm digs its burrow depends upon how wet the soil is.

An earthworm needs to live in damp soil. Otherwise, the sun will dry it out and kill it.

If the ground is damp, an earthworm stays near the surface. If the earth is dry, an earthworm will dig deeper into the ground to find wet soil. An earthworm can dig 8 feet (2 m) down into the ground if it needs to.

Earthworms are nocturnal. This means they sleep during the day and are active at night. They spend the day beneath the earth, safely away from direct sunlight. When the sun goes down, they crawl out of their burrows. They also come out of the ground when there are heavy rains. They may do this because the rain floods their burrows. Earthworms may also surface to find food sources that are knocked loose by rain. When the ground above its burrow freezes in winter, an earthworm curls up into a ball. Earthworms may also gather in large groups under the surface for protection against the cold. They can stay there for long periods of time, as they wait for the ground to soften so they can dig again.

An earthworm will come out of its burrow after heavy rains.

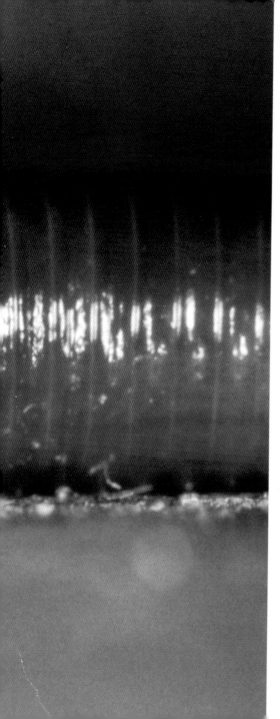

The Earthworm Body

Earthworms are generally reddish or reddish brown in color. The average earthworm is about 0.5 inches (1 cm) wide and 10 to 12 inches (25 to 30 cm) long. The largest earthworms live in Australia. These can stretch 12 feet (4 m) long and weigh 1.5 pounds (0.7 kg). Earthworms are invertebrates. This means they do not have a backbone. In fact, earthworms have no bones at all. An earthworm's body looks like a long, thin tube. The body is soft and flexible. Earthworms can twist and bend, and can even tie themselves into a knot!

The segments that make up an earthworm's body are called annuli. These segments look like rings. Earthworms generally have between 100 and 200 segments. An earthworm has 5 hearts and a brain located at the front end of its body.

Between 100 and 200 segments, or rings, make up an earthworm's body.

It can be hard to tell the front of an earthworm from the back. There are a few ways, though. The front is a bit wider. It is also a lighter color than the back end.

An earthworm's mouth is on the first segment. An earthworm uses its lip to pull food into its mouth. Earthworms do not have teeth to help them chew. But they do have strong mouth muscles that help break up their food. After food is swallowed, the muscles of a digestive organ called a gizzard grind it up. This ground-up food then passes through the earthworm's intestine, which runs through the whole length of the body. Any food the earthworm does not digest is excreted as waste. Waste passes through an opening at the back end of an earthworm.

An intestine runs the whole length of an earthworm's body. Food passes through the intestine to be digested.

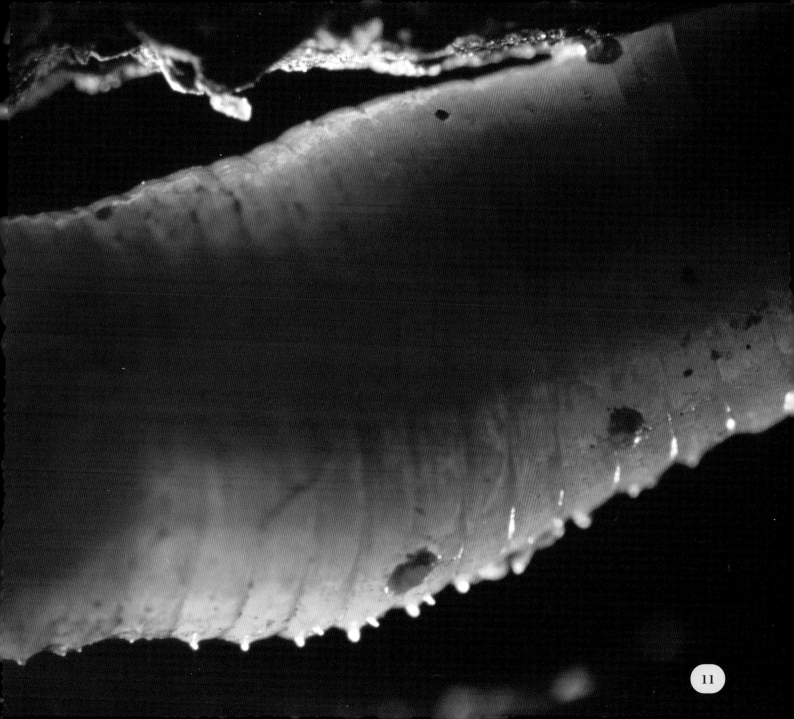

Earthworms cannot see, smell, or hear. But they can sense the vibrations of movement. This lets them know when danger is nearby. Earthworms can also sense light with special cells on their bodies.

An earthworm does not use lungs or gills to breathe. Instead, it breathes by taking in oxygen through its skin. Being wet helps the earthworm absorb oxygen. If an earthworm dries out in the sun, it will die from a lack of oxygen. Earthworms are able to stay moist because they have slippery mucus that coats their bodies. The mucus also helps them slide through the ground more easily. It is this mucus that makes an earthworm feel slimy.

A mucus coating on an earthworm's body helps it to move across the dirt.

How an Earthworm Moves

Earthworms have no legs or feet. To move, they contract, or tighten, the muscles in their bodies. Earthworms have two kinds of muscles. Circular muscles are found around each one of their segments. When an earthworm tightens all of its circular muscles, its body becomes longer and thinner. Earthworms also have longitudinal, or long, muscles. These run along the entire length of the body. When an earthworm tightens its long muscles, its body gets shorter and fatter. By first tightening the circular muscles and then tightening the long muscles, an earthworm moves slowly through the ground.

Each segment of an earthworm (except for the first and last) has four pairs of bristles called setae. There are two pairs of setae on the sides and two pairs on the bottom of each segment. Setae have tiny hooks on the end. The setae help an earthworm pull itself through the soil. They also help it hold onto the earth when it wants to stay in one place.

Gatherers

Because earthworms are nocturnal, they mainly look for food at night. They usually come out of the ground to feed at the surface. Sometimes, an earthworm anchors its back end in its burrow. Then it stretches and wiggles its front end around in the dirt to find food without having to leave home.

Earthworms usually come out of their burrows at night to feed.

Earthworms swallow whatever fits in their tiny mouths. They like to eat leaves and other plant material. They also eat mouthfuls of dirt as they move through the ground. The earth they eat has small pieces of dead insects, leaves, and other plant matter in it. An earthworm digests these nutrients. Anything that the earthworm's body cannot break down, such as pebbles, passes through its body and is left behind.

This earthworm waste is called castings. Castings are actually clumps of dirt that are rich in vitamins and minerals. Castings act as a natural fertilizer. They improve the earth's soil and feed plant life. The average earthworm can deposit a total of 8 pounds (4 kg) of castings in a year. Because earthworms can turn decaying plant matter into rich soil, they are often thought of as nature's recyclers.

Earthworm castings have vitamins and minerals in them that help fertilize soil.

Predators

Earthworms are an important source of food for many animals. That is because their bodies are very high in protein. An earthworm has a variety of predators (animals that hunt other animals for food). These include birds, snakes, toads, skunks, beetles, slugs, and centipedes. Sometimes, humans even dig up earthworms and use them for fish bait.

Earthworms are never safe from predators. They are hunted at night by other nocturnal animals. They are also eaten during the day by diurnal animals (animals that sleep at night and are active during the day). It does not matter where they go, either. Underground creatures such as moles and shrews eat earthworms, as do animals that live above ground, such as frogs and salamanders.

Because so many animals feast on them, earthworms generally only live about a year. But they do have ways to protect themselves. Earthworms can feel vibrations as a predator comes near. If the earthworm feels the vibrations soon enough, it can burrow deeper into the earth and not be eaten.

Earthworms also have another way to save themselves. Sometimes, an animal will tug at an earthworm in order to pull it from the ground and eat it. This tugging may break an earthworm into two pieces. When this happens, there is still a chance that the part of the earthworm left in the ground can live. That is because an earthworm is able to regrow its segments as long as it breaks after the 35th segment.

Turtles are just one of the many animals that eat earthworms.

The Mating Game

Earthworms have both male and female sex organs. Every earthworm makes eggs and sperm. Even so, two worms need to mate with each other in order to reproduce. An earthworm is able to reproduce after it is about 2 to 3 months old. At this time, the worm grows a special body part called a clitellum. This is a thick band that is usually orange or whitish in color. The clitellum is found on an earthworm's body after about the 18th segment from the head.

Earthworms breed at night, and mating usually takes place above ground. During mating, two earthworms lie side by side, with their heads at opposite directions. The clitellum makes a mucus that helps the worms stick together as they mate. The two worms may stay this way for 2 to 3 hours while they exchange sperm cells. The substances produced by the clitellum also form a capsule that will hold the earthworm's eggs.

After mating, this capsule slides along an earthworm's body. As it moves, the capsule gathers the earthworm's eggs and the sperm left by the other earthworm. The capsule then slips over the front end of the earthworm and is left on the ground. It quickly folds into a sealed cocoon, which protects the eggs until they hatch. A milky protein called albumin surrounds the eggs inside the cocoon. Between 1 and 20 eggs will be fertilized.

Babies

Earthworms do not raise their young. Once a cocoon is left on the ground, the earthworm moves on and does not return. After 2 to 4 weeks, the baby worms wriggle out of their cocoon. When they are born, earthworm babies have tiny white bodies. Within a few hours, their color grows darker. The first food they eat is the nutritious albumin from the cocoon. They are able and ready to dig into the ground as soon as they hatch. They go off to burrow and find their own food. Earthworms are fully grown within one year.

Earthworm babies break free of their cocoons after spending 2 to 4 weeks on the ground.

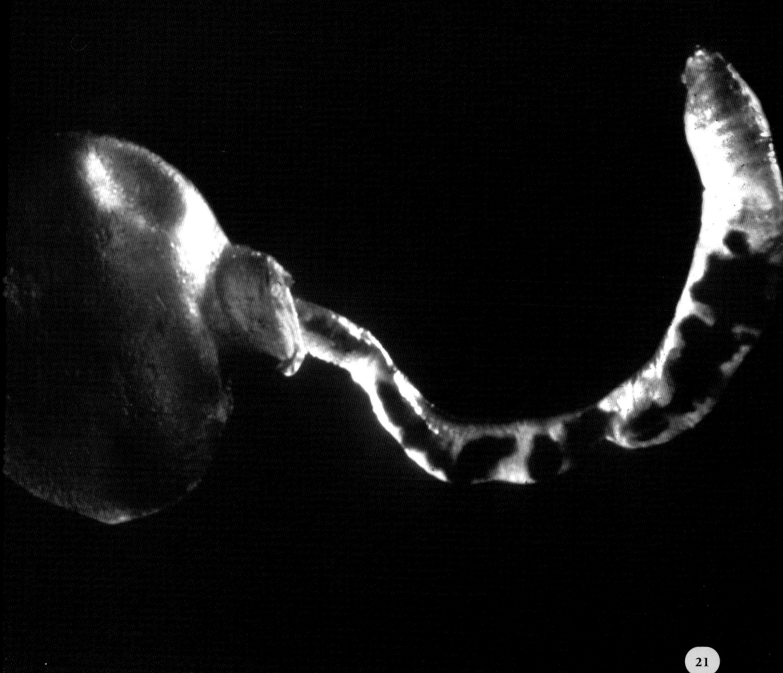

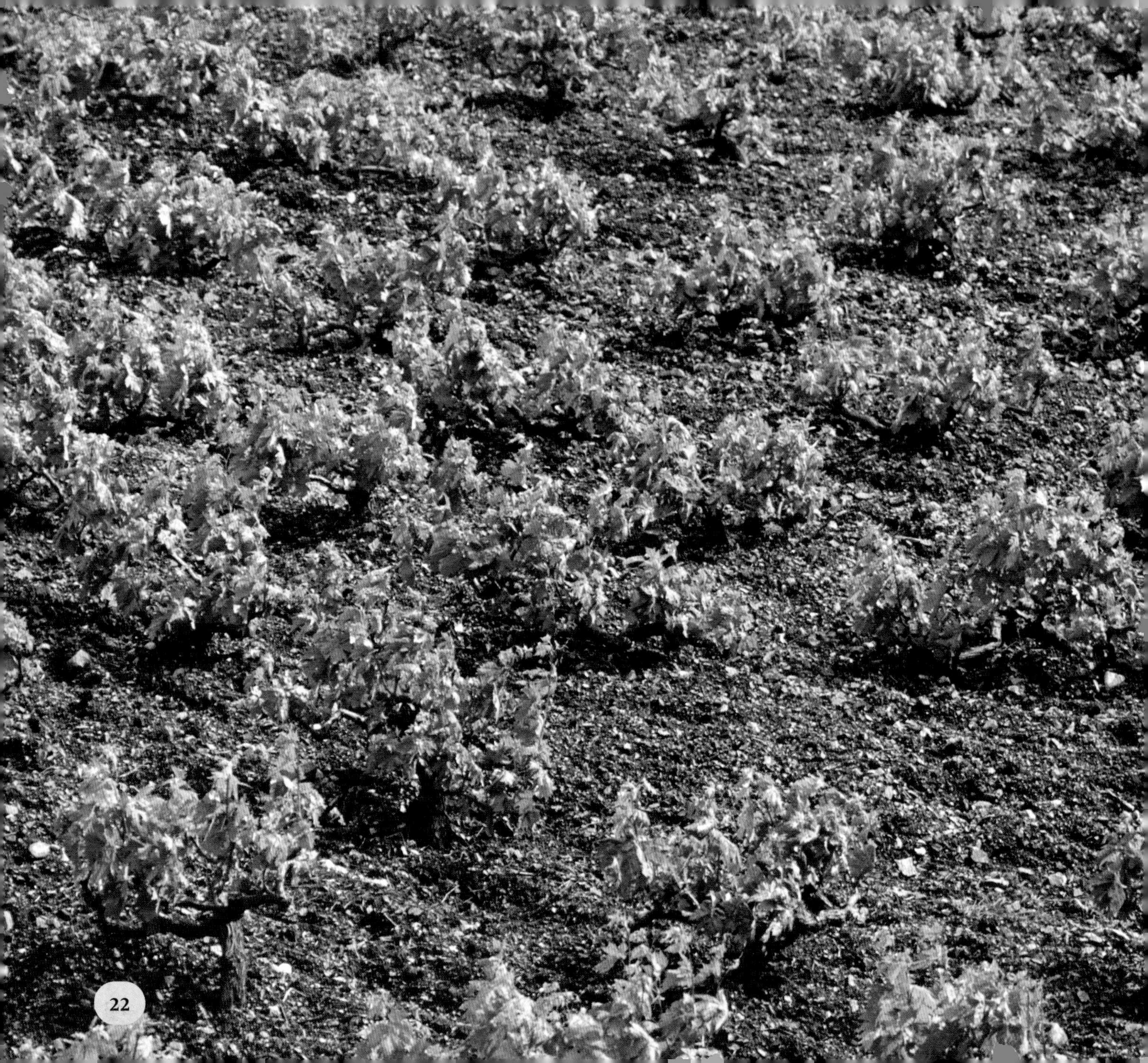

Earthworms and Humans

Farmers and gardeners know that earthworms are good for the earth. They make the land better. Earthworms mix up the soil as they dig their burrows. And the holes in the ground left by the burrows help air and water move through the dirt. All of this movement improves the quality of the soil and helps many kinds of plants to grow. Earthworms are part of nature's clean-up crew. They turn old bits of plants into rich soil. Gardeners also use earthworms and their castings to make their gardens healthier. Humans, plants, and animals all benefit from earthworms' behavior and habits.

Earthworm movement and waste help to create a rich soil that is ideal for growing healthy gardens.

Glossary

annuli ringlike segments of an earthworm

castings waste products of earthworms

diurnal asleep at night and active during the day

invertebrate an animal that has no backbone

mucus a slippery coating on a worm's body

nocturnal asleep during the day and active at night

predator an animal that hunts other animals for food

setae small bristles on the segments of an earthworm

For Further Reading

Lauber, Patricia. *Earthworms: Underground Farmers*. New York: Henry Holt, 1994.

Merrick, Patrick. *Earthworms*. (Naturebook series). Chanhassen, MN: Child's World, 1999.

Pascoe, Elaine. *Earthworms*. (Nature Close-Up series). San Diego, CA: Blackbirch Press, 1997.

Index